Sunshine Coast Seafood

A collection of recipes using locally available seafood.

By

Grace Taylor
Wendy Rogers
Lauren Armstrong

Arbutus Bay Publications

Second Printing : February 1986

Arbutus Bay Publications
#12 (Jolly) Secret Cove
RR #1 Halfmoon Bay, British Columbia
Canada VON 1Y0

Printed By Friesen Printers

Hand Lettering and Art Work by
Wendy Rogers
Cover Design by Mineo Morimoto
and Wendy Rogers
First Printing : September 1985
Canadian Cataloguing in Publication
Data:

Taylor, Grace 1936
Sunshine Coast Seafood

Includes Index
ISBN 0-88925-621-7

1. Cookery (Seafood) 1. Rogers, Wendy,
1959 - 2. Armstrong, Lauren, 1958 -
3. Title. TX747.T39 1985 641.6'92
C85-091383-7

Table of Contents

About This Book

Three people have been involved in the creation of this cookbook: Grace Taylor and her daughters, Wendy Rogers and Lauren Armstrong.

A love for the Sunshine Coast and the cooking of fresh seafood from local salt waters led to this presentation of a strictly seafood cookbook.

Many residents from the area (Gibsons to Powell River, B.C.) have also contributed. The result is a wide variety of seafood cookery.

Points to remember when cooking seafood:
1. Use the freshest possible seafood.
2. Do not overcook.
3. Feel free to experiment with the recipes — adjust ingredients to suit your own taste.

Enjoy!

Grace Taylor

Wendy Rogers

Lauren Armstrong

Ousters Crab

Oysters

Crab

Baked Oysters Creole

Oven 450°F - 15-20 mins.
Serves 4

This is a delicious appetizer cooked in individual ramekins.

¼ cup butter
¼ cup olive oil
⅔ cup bread crumbs
salt and pepper to taste
⅛ tsp. cayenne
½ tsp. tarragon
½ tsp. oregano
2 tbsp. fresh parsley, chopped
2 cloves garlic, minced
3 tbsp. green onions, chopped
2 dozen oysters, drained

1. Melt the butter in heavy saucepan. Add the olive oil and heat.
2. Add all the other ingredients except the oysters. Mix well and remove from heat.
3. Place the well drained oysters in individual ramekins and pour equal portions of the sauce over each.
4. Bake in 450° oven for 15-20 mins., until topping is browned.

Myrtle Point Oyster Bisque

Serves 4

This is a fool-proof recipe but you must use a double boiler to prevent over cooking.

2 tbsp. green onion, chopped
1 clove garlic, minced
½ cup celery, chopped
4 tbsp. butter
1½ pints oysters with liquor
1½ cups milk
½ cup cream
salt and pepper
2 egg yolks, beaten
2 tbsp. fresh parsley, chopped

1. Sauté lightly the onion, garlic and celery in butter. Place in double boiler over boiling water.
2. Add oysters with liquor, milk, cream, salt and pepper to taste. Cook until the milk is hot and the oysters float.
3. Remove from heat. Add a small amount to the egg yolks and mix. Now add yolks slowly to the

cont'd...

Continued

hot milk. Reheat for 1 min. but do not allow to boil or the bisque will curdle.

4. Add the parsley and serve.

Oven 450°F - 5-7 mins.
Serves 2

This baked oyster dish is one of the easiest to prepare. The combination of bacon, green pepper and pimiento is dramatic and delicious.

Prepare the rock salt and oysters on the half shell as directed in the recipe for Oysters Bienville.

1 dozen oysters on the half shell, drained
4 pans rock salt
2 slices bacon, chopped
2 tbsp. butter
2/3 cup green pepper, chopped
2 tsp. pimiento
juice of 1 lemon
salt and pepper

1. In a small heavy pan fry the bacon until not quite crisp. Add the butter.

cont'd ...

2. Add the green pepper, pimiento, lemon juice, salt and pepper to taste and cook for 5-7 mins. until the green pepper is soft but not browned.
3. Spoon over the oysters on the half shell. Place shells on the hot rock salt and bake in 450° oven until bubbly. Serve immediately.

Oysters Bienville

Oven 450°F – 15-20 mins.
Serves 4

These fresh oysters, baked on the half shell with a rich sauce, are far less complicated to prepare than you may expect.

2 dozen oysters on the half shell, drained
4 pans rock salt

Bienville Sauce

½ cup butter
1 cup green onions, finely chopped
¼ cup fresh parsley, chopped
½ cup flour
½ cup whipping cream
1½ cup milk
4 egg yolks, beaten
¼ cup dry sherry
salt and pepper
½ tsp. cayenne
⅔ cup fresh mushrooms, chopped
½ pound shrimp, finely chopped

cont'd ...

1. Melt the butter over low heat in a heavy saucepan.
2. Add the onions, parsley and garlic and simmer for 10 mins.
3. Gradually add the flour and stir until smooth.
4. Add the cream and milk slowly, stirring until smooth.
5. Add the egg yolks, sherry, salt and pepper to taste and cayenne. Cook over low heat until the mixture begins to thicken.
6. Add the shrimp and mushrooms and cook until the sauce is quite thick, about 5 mins. Cool and refrigerate until ready to use.
7. Preheat the pans of rock salt in 500° oven for 30 mins.
8. Pour 1 heaping tablespoon of the sauce over each oyster on the half shell. Place shells on the hot rock salt and bake in 450° oven for 15-20 mins.

A topping of bread crumbs, grated cheese and paprika can be sprinkled over each sauced oyster before baking.

Oysters Rockefeller

Oven 450°F - 15 mins.
Serves 4

This is an old favourite, and is easy to prepare.

2 dozen oysters on the half shell, drained
4 pans rock salt

Rockefeller Sauce

1 cup butter, softened
1 cup cooked spinach, finely chopped
½ cup green onions, chopped
¼ cup fresh parsley, chopped
2 tbsp. celery, finely chopped
salt and pepper to taste
½ tsp. marjoram
½ tsp. basil
½ tsp. cayenne
2 tbsp. pernod (optional)

1. Combine all the ingredients. Form into oval patties about 2 tbsp. each.
2. Preheat the rock salt.
3. Place a pattie on each oyster on half shell. Place shells on rock salt.

cont'd...

Bake in 450° oven for 15 mins. until the sauce bubbles and is slightly browned on top. Allow to cool for about 5 mins. before serving.

Sautéed Oysters

Serves 2

12 shucked oysters
2 eggs, beaten
1 cup fine bread crumbs
3 tbsp. butter
salt and pepper

1. Pat the oysters dry between paper towels.
2. Dip each oyster in the egg and then in the cracker crumbs. Repeat this process.
3. Melt butter in skillet over medium heat. Add the oysters and cook about 3 mins. on each side, or until golden. Sprinkle with salt and pepper to taste.

Serve as an appetizer with lemon wedges.

Crab Mousse

This is good served as an appetizer.

1 envelope unflavoured gelatin
1/4 cup water, cold
1/2 cup boiling water
1/2 cup mayonnaise
3 tbsp. chives, chopped
1 tsp. fresh dill, finely chopped
1 tbsp. onion, finely chopped
1 tbsp. lemon juice
dash of tobasco sauce
1 tsp. salt
2 cups crabmeat
1 cup whipping cream
fresh dill or parsley

1. Add the gelatin to the cold water, stir and let stand for 3 mins. Stir in the boiling water and stir until the gelatin dissolves. Cool to room temperature.
2. Stir in all the ingredients except the crabmeat and cream. Refrigerate until slightly thickened about 15-20 mins.
3. Fold the crabmeat into the gelatin mixture.

cont'd...

4. Whip the cream until it forms soft peaks. Gently fold into the crab mixture.
5. Place the mixture in a serving dish or a mold. Refrigerate for 3-4 hours or until set.

Garnish with parsley or dill. Serve with assorted crackers.

Crabmeat and Proscuitto Ham

Preheat the broiler
Serves 6

This is a very versatile recipe. You may substitute shrimp for the crabmeat. Also, a hollandaise sauce or grated cheese may be used as a topping before broiling.

4 tbsp. butter
2 tbsp. onion, chopped
2 tbsp. fresh parsley, chopped
1½ to 2 cups fresh Dungeness crabmeat
salt and pepper
6 slices proscuitto ham

1. Melt butter in a pan, add onions and cook until tender. Add the crabmeat and cook only to heat through. Add salt and pepper to taste.
2. Divide crabmeat mixture in 6 equal portions onto each slice of ham. Roll up and place on baking pan.
3. Broil about 6 inches from heat, until ham is heated.

Crabmeat Salad

Serves 6

Great for a summer luncheon.

2 cups crabmeat
3/4 cup celery, chopped
4 green onions, chopped
1/4 cup fresh parsley, finely chopped
1/4 cup mayonnaise
1 tbsp. dijon style mustard
1/4 cup heavy cream, whipped
2 tbsp. slivered almonds, toasted
salt and pepper

1. Combine the crabmeat, celery, onion and parsley in a bowl and chill.
2. Mix the mayonnaise and mustard in a small bowl. Fold in the whipped cream.
3. Add the mayonnaise dressing to the crabmeat mixture. Season with salt and pepper to taste and stir. Serve on individual plates lined with lettuce. Sprinkle almonds overall.

Serve with crusty rolls and a dry white wine.

Crab Stuffed Mushroom Caps

Oven 350°F - 5-10 mins.

24 large mushrooms
8 ounces cream cheese
1 tbsp. sherry
4 ounces crabmeat
2 tbsp. onions, finely chopped
½ tsp. worcestershire sauce
½ tsp. lemon juice
salt and pepper
2 tbsp. butter, melted

1. Remove stems from mushrooms and dice. Place the mushroom caps on a buttered baking sheet.
2. Combine diced stems and all above ingredients except the butter. Fill the mushroom caps. Drizzle with the butter. Bake in 350° oven for 5-10 mins.

SUNSHINE COAST
GOLF AND COUNTRY CLUB

Crab Zucchini Bake

Oven 375°F - 30 mins.
Serves 4

4 tbsp. butter
1 small onion, chopped
3 small zucchini, unpeeled and sliced
1 clove garlic, minced
3 large tomatoes, chopped
1/2 pound crabmeat
1 1/3 cups Swiss Gruyère cheese, grated
1 cup fine breadcrumbs
salt and pepper to taste
1/4 tsp. basil, crushed
paprika

1. Melt butter in large pan and add the onion, zucchini and garlic. Sauté until the onion is transparent. Remove from heat.
2. Add the tomatoes, crab, 1 cup of the cheese, 3/4 cup of the breadcrumbs, salt and pepper and basil.
3. Place the mixture into a shallow baking dish. Sprinkle the top with the remaining cheese and breadcrumbs. Dot with additional butter. Sprinkle with paprika. Bake uncovered in 375° oven for 30 mins. Serve hot.

Davis Bay Crab Imperial

Oven 350°F – 15 mins.
Serves 8

1 green pepper, finely diced
1 tbsp. dijon style mustard
1 tsp. salt
½ tsp. white pepper
2 eggs
1 cup mayonnaise
3 pounds crabmeat, whole pieces
paprika

1. Mix together the green pepper, mustard, salt, pepper, eggs and mayonnaise. Add crabmeat and mix lightly so that the pieces are not broken.
2. Divide the mixture into 8 scallop shells or ramekins.
3. Coat the tops with a little mayonnaise and sprinkle with paprika.
4. Bake in 350° oven for 15 mins. Serve hot.

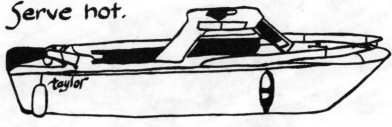

Gower Point Crab Dip

1 can crabmeat, drained
1 cup sour cream
½ cup mayonnaise
1 tbsp. green onion, finely chopped
1 tbsp. horseradish
2 tbsp. fresh parsley, chopped
1 tsp. dijon style mustard
⅛ tsp. Worcestershire sauce
4 drops tabasco sauce
salt and pepper to taste.

Mix all ingredients in a bowl. Refrigerate for 2-3 hours. Serve with assorted crackers.

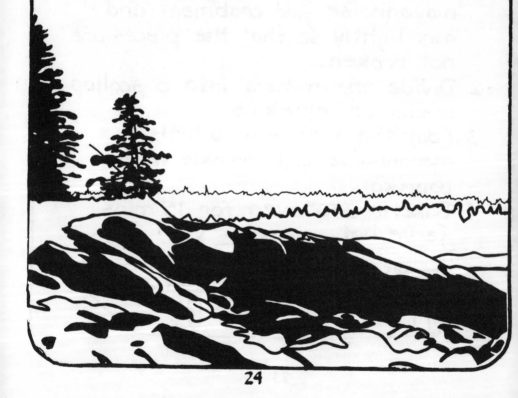

Pender Harbour Crab Paté

Oven 300°F – 15 mins.

6 ounces crab , drained
8 ounces cream cheese
¼ tsp. dry mustard
1 tsp. onion , grated
1 tsp. horseradish

Combine the above ingredients.
Bake in 300° oven for 15 mins.

Serve hot. Dip with small
crackers.

Scotch Crab Soup

Serves 4

3 tbsp. butter
2 tbsp. onion, finely chopped
2 cups crabmeat
salt and pepper
3 cups milk
½ cup whipping cream
2 tbsp. scotch
parsley and paprika

1. Melt the butter in a pan and add the onion and cook until wilted. Stir in the crabmeat and salt and pepper to taste, and simmer for 2 mins.
2. Place the crabmeat mixture in the top of a double boiler over simmering water. Add the milk and cook, stirring occasionally for 15mins. Blend in the cream. When the mixture is hot, stir in the scotch. Sprinkle with parsley and paprika and serve.

Secret Cove Crab Quiche

Oven 375°F – 35 mins.
Serves 4-6

1 cup onion, sliced thin
1 tbsp. butter
1 cup Swiss Gruyère cheese, grated
1 cup crab
4 eggs
½ cup whipping cream
1 tbsp. flour
⅛ tsp. nutmeg
salt and pepper
1 tbsp. butter, melted

1. Bake 9 inch pie shell for 15 mins.
2. Cook onions in butter until soft. Place in pie shell. Add cheese.
3. Combine crab, eggs, cream, flour, nutmeg and salt and pepper and beat lightly. Pour over the cheese.
4. Pour butter over top and bake in 375° oven for 35 mins.

Sherried Crab and Artichokes

Oven 350°F - 30 mins.
Serves 6

This casserole may be made early in the day, refrigerated and baked for your luncheon or evening party.

1¼ cups macaroni shells, cooked to package directions
2 cups fresh crabmeat
4 tbsp. butter
¼ cup flour
2 green onions, chopped
3¼ cups light cream or milk
⅓ cup sherry
1 can (8 oz.) artichoke hearts, drained
1 cup fresh mushrooms, sliced
¼ cup parmesan cheese, grated
paprika

1. Melt butter in a pan. Stir In the flour until smooth. Add the onions.
2. Stir in the cream gradually. Bring just to a boil and then simmer for 5 mins., stirring. Then remove from heat.

cont'd...

3. Cook macaroni and drain.
4. Combine the crabmeat, sherry, macaroni, artichokes and mushrooms with the sauce. Place in a baking dish. Top with the parmesan cheese and sprinkle with paprika.
5. Bake in 350° oven for 30 mins. or until heated through.

Serve with hot rolls and salad.

Oven 400° – 6 mins.

A classic method of serving oysters.

Cut each slice of bacon into 2 pieces. Fry until limp.

Wrap bacon around oyster and secure with a toothpick. Place an baking sheet and cook for about 3 mins. on each side until the bacon is crisp.

Serve on snacktray.

Shrimp

Prawns

Shrimp and Artichoke Supreme

Oven 375°F - 20 mins.
Serves 4

Perfect for entertaining - your friends will enjoy this gourmet dish.

6 tbsp. butter
3 tbsp. flour
2 cups. milk, warmed
salt and pepper to taste
1/2 tsp. thyme
1/2 tsp. worchestershire sauce
dash of tobasco sauce
1/4 cup dry sherry
1 can (14 oz.) artichoke hearts
1 pound fresh shrimpmeat
1 cup fresh mushrooms, sliced
1/4 cup parmesan cheese, grated
paprika

1. Melt 4 tbsp. butter in saucepan. Blend in the flour. Slowly add the warm milk. Boil for 1 min. and then simmer for 15 mins., stirring.
2. Add the seasonings and the sherry. Remove from the heat.

cont'd...

3. Drain the artichokes, cut in half and arrange in a shallow buttered casserole dish. Place the shrimp on top of the artichokes.
4. Saute the mushrooms in 2 tbsp. butter and pour over the shrimp.
5. Pour the sauce overall. Sprinkle with cheese and paprika. Bake in 375° oven for 20 mins.

Serve with a green salad and a dry white wine.

Penny Rogers, Vancouver.

Serves 4

½ cup butter
1 medium onion, chopped
3 cloves garlic, minced
2 tbsp. flour
1 cup water
1 celery stick, whole
1 can (10 oz.) tomato sauce
6 drops tobasco sauce
2 bay leaves
½ tsp. thyme
¼ tsp. pepper
1 pound shrimp, shelled
Garnish: 2 green onions and 2 hard boiled eggs

1. Melt the butter in a pan. Add the onions and garlic and cook until tender. Stir in the flour. Add the water and blend.
2. Add all the ingredients except the shrimp. Simmer for 25 mins. Remove the celery stick.
3. Add the shrimp to the sauce and simmer for 15 mins. Serve over rice. Sprinkle with green onion and hard boiled eggs.

— Lin Morrison, Powell River

Shrimp Marinière

This may be made in individual dishes or in a casserole.

1 pound shrimp, shelled
3 tbsp. butter
2 green onions, chopped
2 tsp. flour
1 cup fish or chicken broth
2 tbsp. fresh mushrooms, sliced
1 tbsp. fresh parsley, chopped
2 ounces dry white wine
salt and pepper to taste
bread crumbs

1. Sauté shrimp and onions in butter for 2 to 3 mins.
2. Blend in flour and gradually stir in the broth.
3. Add remaining ingredients except the bread crumbs. Simmer for 3 to 5 mins.
4. Pour into casserole dish, sprinkle with bread crumbs and place under broiler until golden.

Shrimp Paté

1½ cups cooked shrimp
¼ cup dry white wine
2 tbsp shallots, minced
1 package cream cheese (4 ounces)
1 tsp. dijon style mustard
⅓ cup butter, softened

1. Rinse shrimp, drain and pat dry. Chop shrimp, add shallots, and combine with wine.
2. Beat cheese to soften. Add mustard and butter and beat until creamy. Add shrimp mixture and combine.
3. Place in serving container. Cover and chill.

This mixture can be made into a ball and rolled in finely chopped fresh parsley or sprinkled with paprika.

Serve with cocktail crackers.

Shrimp Seviche

Serves 6

This is a very colourful served at a buffet cocktail party.

½ pound fresh shrimp, cooked and
    shelled
2 tbsp. olive oil
½ cup lime juice
2 cloves garlic, minced
¼ tsp. red pepper flakes
6 peppercorns
1 medium onion, sliced
several bay leaves

1. Mix the olive oil, lime juice, garlic, red pepper flakes and peppercorns.
2. In a wide-mouth jar alternate layers of shrimp, onion and bay leaves. Pour the marinade overall.
3. Put the lid on the jar and place jar on its side in the refrigerator. Turn occasionally. Marinate for at least 12 hours. Drain and serve in a glass bowl with cocktail picks.

Shrimp Vol - au - vent

Yields 24

Appetizers at a moment's notice.

1 package frozen vol-au-vent shells
2 - 4 ounce cans cocktail shrimp
1/4 cup mayonnaise
1/4 cup sour cream
1 tsp. lemon juice
parsley or fresh dill

1. Bake shells according to package directions. Cool.
2. Combine remaining ingredients and spoon into shells. Garnish with parsley or fresh dill and serve.

Spicy Shrimp Creole

Serves 4

This is a really spicy Cajun dish. You may want to reduce the cayenne a touch the first time you try it.

2 pounds whole fresh shrimp, shelled
boiled rice

Hot Sauce

2/3 cup vegetable oil
1/2 cup flour
2 cups onion, chopped
1/3 cup celery, chopped
4 cloves garlic, minced
3 tbsp. fresh parsley, chopped
1 can (16 oz.) Italian Style tomatoes, drained
1 can (8 oz.) tomato sauce
4 tbsp. dry red wine
4 whole bay leaves, crushed
2 whole cloves
2 tsp. salt
3/4 tsp. pepper

cont'd...

½ tsp. cayenne
¼ tsp. chili powder
¼ tsp. mace
¼ tsp. basil
½ tsp. thyme
4 tsp. lemon juice
2 cups water

1. In a large pot heat the oil and gradually add flour. Cook over medium heat, stirring until golden brown.
2. Reduce heat and add the chopped vegetables. Cook slightly
3. Mix in the tomatoes, tomato sauce, wine, seasonings, lemon juice and water. Bring to boil, reduce heat and simmer for 45 mins.
4. Add the shrimp and cook for 3 to 5 mins.

Serve over boiled rice.

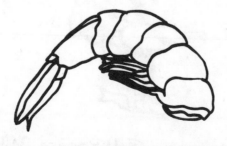

Bill's Garlic Prawns

Serves 4

2 pounds raw prawns, heads and shells on
3 tbsp. butter
3 tbsp. olive oil
garlic salt to taste

1. Wash and drain the prawns.
2. Heat the butter and olive oil in large pan until bubbly but not brown.
3. Cover the bottom of the pan with prawns and sprinkle with garlic salt. Turn prawns frequently until pink.
4. Serve to guests. They do the work of shelling and eating.

Bill Rogers, White Rock

Garlic Finger Prawns

Serves 4

Have finger bowls and napkins ready for this informal dish. Your guests will love it.

2 pounds large prawns, headless
2 bay leaves, crushed
⅛ tsp. oregano
⅛ tsp. rosemary
salt and pepper to taste
5 or 6 cloves garlic, minced
4 tbsp. olive oil
2 tbsp. dry white wine
lemon wedges

1. Wash and drain the prawns and pat dry with paper towels.
2. Place all the ingredients except wine in a pan and sauté over medium heat for 5 mins., stirring constantly.
3. Add wine and cook until it boils, about 1 min.
4. Serve in shells, along with finger bowls and lemon wedges.

Prawns Grand Marnier

2 tbsp. olive oil
1 clove garlic, minced
1 medium onion, finely chopped
1 pound prawns in shells
2 tbsp. white wine
juice of ½ lemon
2 tbsp. Grand Marnier
6 sprigs fresh parsley, finely chopped

1. Heat oil in frying pan. Add garlic and onions and cook until the onions are transparent.
2. Add the prawns, wine and lemon juice. Stir until prawns turn pink, about 5 mins.
3. Add Grand Marnier and flambé. Sprinkle with parsley and serve on a bed of rice.

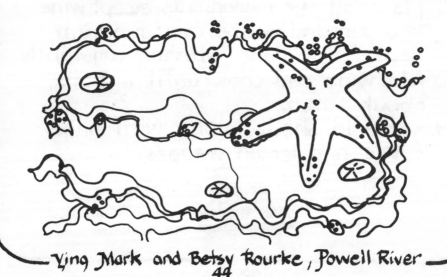

Ying Mark and Betsy Rourke, Powell River

Sautéed Prawns

Serves 2

1 dozen large prawns, peeled
2 tbsp. butter
1 tbsp. celery, chopped
1 tbsp. green pepper, chopped
1 tbsp. onion, chopped
1 tbsp. fresh parsley, chopped
1 clove garlic, minced
2 tbsp. lemon juice
1 tsp. worcestershire sauce

1. Sauté all the ingredients except the shrimp 3-4 mins.
2. Add shrimp and cook 5-6 mins.

Serve with salad and hot rolls.

Microwave 2-3 mins.
Serves 2

1 pound large prawns, heads and
  shells on
melted garlic butter

1. Place in microwave on high power
   for 2-3 mins. until pink.
2. Serve with a small dish of garlic
   butter for dipping.

Salmon

Halibut

Serves 6

One of the easiest and most delicious ways to cook fresh salmon. Serve with hollandaise sauce.

6 salmon steaks, 3/4 inch thick
2 tsp. salt
2 tbsp. wine vinegar
parsley sprigs

1. Place about 4 inches of water in roast pan. Bring to a boil and add the salt and vinegar. Lay the salmon in pan and simmer (do not boil) for 8 mins. Turn off the heat. You may let it stand for a few minutes while you prepare the sauce.

Serve with hollandaise sauce.

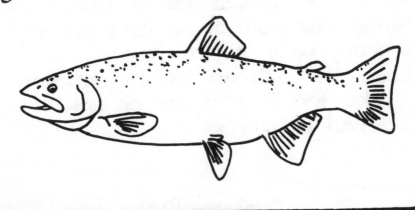

Joe's Smoked Salmon

This method works well with previously frozen salmon. Use a Little Chief Smoker.

Brine:

6 cups water
½ cup coarse salt
½ cup sugar
1 tsp. garlic powder
1 tsp. pepper
1 tsp. onion powder
3 bay leaves
2-3 small coho or spring salmon,

1. Combine all the ingredients to make the brine.
2. Soak the salmon in the brine for 4 or more hours. A 5 pound salmon should be soaked for 8 hours.
3. Rinse the salmon in cold water and dry with paper towels.
4. Load the salmon in the smoker. Smoke for 4 - 5 hours or until desired doneness.

Lasqueti Salmon Steaks

Barbeque
Serves 4

4 salmon steaks, 1 inch thick
½ cup dry vermouth
¼ cup butter, melted
2 tbsp. lemon juice
2 tbsp. onions, finely chopped
salt and pepper to taste
⅛ tsp. marjoram
⅛ tsp. thyme
1 clove garlic, minced

1. Combine the marinade ingredients and pour over the salmon in a shallow dish. Marinate for 2 hours, basting occasionally.
2. Place steaks in a wire grill and barbeque about 4 inches from the hot coals. Baste during cooking with the marinade. Barbeque about 8-10 mins. or until salmon flakes with a fork.

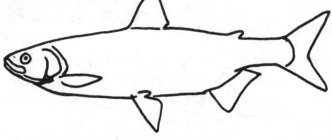

Ole's Cove Barbequed Salmon

Barbeque
Serves 4

1 - 3 pound salmon, filleted
¼ cup butter
1 tbsp. lemon juice
1 clove garlic, minced
2 tbsp. parsley
pepper and salt to taste

1. Place fillets, skin side down on tinfoil.
2. Melt butter, add remaining ingredients and stir. Brush marinade over the salmon.
3. Place on gas barbeque, close lid and cook until flakey.

Serve with wild rice for an appetizing addition.

Seviche - Pickled Salmon

Serves 6

This is a Mexican style of pickling salmon. It keeps for 1 week in the fridge.

2-3 pounds salmon fillets
8 ounces lime juice
1 large onion, thinly sliced
3 bay leaves
1 cup white vinegar
10 whole peppercorns
¼ tsp. cayenne
1 tbsp. pickling salt
1 tbsp. brown sugar
2 tbsp. olive oil
2 whole dried red chili pods

1. Place the salmon in a deep dish. Mix the remaining ingredients and pour over the salmon. Cover and refrigerate for 24 hours, basting occasionally.
2. Slice thin strips and serve with the onion and crackers.

Skookumchuk Salmon Pasta

Serves 6

An excellent brunch dish using leftover baked or poached salmon.

1 pound pasta (or fresh spinach pasta)
3 tbsp. butter
2 cups cream
pinch of thyme
salt and pepper to taste
1 tbsp. parmesan cheese, grated
2 cups flaked cooked salmon
parsley or fresh dill

1. Cook the pasta according to package directions. Drain and toss with butter. Set aside.
2. Simmer the cream, thyme, salt and pepper until the cream is reduced by about one quarter. Add the parmesan, salmon and parsley or dill. Stir and remove from heat.
3. Place pasta on plates, cover with the sauce and serve.

Smoked Salmon Paté

Yields 2 cups

8 ounces cream cheese, room temperature
¼ cup whipping cream
1 green onion, finely chopped
1 tsp. lemon juice
dash of tobasco sauce
¼ pound smoked salmon, flaked

1. Mix the cream cheese and whipping cream in a bowl. Stir in the onion, lemon juice and tobasco sauce. Gently fold in the salmon.

Serve with assorted crackers.

Baked Halibut

Oven 350°F - 40 mins.
Serves 4

This is an excellent way to cook frozen halibut steaks.

1 pound frozen halibut steaks
1 tbsp. butter
salt and pepper to taste
1 clove garlic, minced
¼ tsp. oregano
¼ tsp. thyme
1 bay leaf
1 medium onion, thinly sliced
½ cup light cream

1. Place frozen halibut in baking dish. Dot with butter and sprinkle with seasonings.
2. Arrange onion on top of the halibut and pour cream overall. Bake in 350° oven for 40 mins., or until the fish flakes with a fork.

Brew Bay Barbequed Halibut

Barbeque
Serves 4

Individual foil packages serve as the baking dish for this delicious barbequed halibut.

4 small halibut steaks, 1 inch thick
2 tbsp. butter
4 green onions, chopped
1 cup fresh mushrooms, sliced
salt and pepper to taste
2 cloves garlic, minced
4 bay leaves
pinch of basil and thyme
1 lemon, sliced
1 medium onion, sliced
¼ cup vermouth or dry white wine

1. Arrange halibut on 4 squares of aluminum foil. Dot with butter and sprinkle with green onions, mushrooms and garlic. Place fish on top. Fold edges of foil up to form individual pans.
2. Add salt, pepper, herbs, sliced onion rings and sprinkle vermouth overall.

cont'd...

3. Place foil packages on the barbeque over hot coals and close lid. Cook for 10-15 mins. or until the fish flakes.

Barbeque
Serves 4

Use your imagination and add other goodies to the skewers.

1½ pounds halibut
1 can (8 oz.) pineapple chunks
16 large mushrooms (parboiled so they don't split)
⅓ cup lemon juice
⅓ cup olive oil
salt and pepper to taste
3 tbsp. fresh parsley, finely chopped
1 tsp. worcestershire sauce
1 clove garlic, minced
1 tsp. dijon style mustard

1. Cut the halibut into 1 inch cubes. Thread fish, pineapple and mushrooms onto skewers.
2. Combine the remaining ingredients. Baste the brochettes liberally with the sauce.
3. Place the brochettes on barbeque, turning frequently and basting for a total of 10 mins.

Mackie's Gourmet Halibut

Oven 450°F - 7-10 mins.
Serves 4

A quick method of preparing halibut.

2 halibut steaks, 1 inch thick
2 green onions, chopped
salt and pepper to taste
½ tsp. thyme
1 clove garlic, minced
½ cup fine breadcrumbs
4 tbsp. butter, melted

1. Butter the bottom of a baking dish. Sprinkle the onion in dish. Arrange the steaks in the dish and sprinkle with salt, pepper, thyme and garlic.
2. Add the breadcrumbs and drizzle the butter overall. Bake in 450° oven for 7-10 mins. Do not over cook.

Gerry Mackie, North Delta

Piquant Baked Halibut

Oven 450°F – 10-15 mins.
Serves 4

Halibut is at its best when fresh, but frozen steaks, defrosted and patted dry are also excellent for this recipe.

3 green onions, chopped
1 green pepper, chopped
½ sweet red pepper, chopped
2 halibut steaks, 1 inch thick
salt and pepper
2 ripe tomatoes, chopped
1 lemon, sliced
½ cup dry white wine
2 tbsp. vermouth (optional)
½ cup clam juice
2 tbsp. butter, melted
parsley and chives

1. Butter baking dish. Sprinkle the onions, green pepper and red pepper on bottom of the dish. Arrange the steaks on top. Add salt and pepper to taste and cover with tomatoes and lemon slices.

cont'd ...

2. Combine the wine, vermouth and clam juice and pour overall.
3. Bake in 450° oven for 10-15 mins. or until the fish flakes. Do not overcook or it will be dry.
4. Pour butter over the halibut and garnish with parsley and chives.

Serve with rice and a green salad.

Sole Cod
Flounder
Red Snapper

63

Sole Flounder

Red Snapper

Cod

Sole Fillets – Halfmoon Bay

Oven 450°F – 15 mins.
Serves 4

2-2½ pounds fillets of sole
4 green onions, chopped
2 tbsp. fresh parsley, chopped
8 fresh mushrooms, sliced
salt and pepper
½ cup dry white wine
1 tbsp. butter, melted
3 tbsp. light cream
1 tsp. lemon juice
1 tbsp. butter

1. Butter a large baking dish.
   Sprinkle the onion and parsley on
   the bottom of dish.
2. Lay the fillets in a single layer
   and sprinkle with mushrooms and
   salt and pepper to taste.
3. Add the wine and top with 1 tbsp.
   butter.
4. Cover dish loosely with aluminum
   foil and bake in 450° oven for
   15 mins., or until fish flakes.

cont'd...

5. Spoon off liquid and reduce in saucepan over high heat.
6. When reduced to half, add hot cream, lemon juice and 1 tbsp. butter. Stir and pour over the fish.
7. Place under broiler until lightly browned.

Serve with small boiled potatoes and a salad.

Sole Florentine

2 pounds sole fillets
salt and pepper
3/4 cup sour cream
1/3 cup mayonnaise
1 tbsp. flour
2 tbsp. lemon juice
1/4 tsp. coriander
1 1/2 pounds fresh spinach
paprika and lemon wedges

1. Season the fillets with salt and
   pepper to taste and place in a
   shallow baking dish.
2. In a small bowl blend the sour cream,
   mayonnaise, flour, lemon juice and
   coriander. Spread this over the fish.
3. Bake in 400° oven for 10 mins. or
   until the fish flakes.
4. Cook the spinach in a pot until just
   wilted, about 4 mins.
5. Place the spinach on a platter. Put
   the fillets on top. Sprinkle with
   paprika and serve with lemon wedges.

Flounder with Dijon Sauce

Preheat the broiler.
Serves 2

1 pound flounder or sole fillets
½ cup mayonnaise
2 tbsp. parmesan cheese, grated
salt and pepper to taste

1. Mix all the ingredients except the fillets. Spread the mixture over the fillets.
2. Broil the fillets for 4-7 mins., depending on the thickness of the fish; until the fish flakes with a fork.

Serve hot with salad and a rice dish.

Savory Shrimp Stuffed Flounder

Oven 400°F - 20 mins.
Serves 6

1 tbsp. butter
4 tbsp. green onion, chopped
2 tbsp. fresh parsley, finely chopped
1/2 pound fresh shelled shrimp
6 flounder fillets, or sole
1/2 cup dry white wine
1 cup cream
4 drops tobasco sauce
1 tsp. lemon juice
salt and pepper

1. Butter the bottom of a baking dish.
   Scatter the onions and 1 tbsp. parsley
   on the bottom.
2. Roll the shrimp in the fillets and
   place in dish seam side down.
3. Mix the wine, cream, tobasco sauce,
   lemon juice, parsley and salt and
   pepper together and pour overall.
4. Bake in 400° oven for 20 mins.

   Note: Mushroom soup may be
   substituted for cream.

Broiled Red Snapper Dijon

Preheat the broiler
Serves 4

1½ pounds red snapper, fillets
½ cup mayonnaise
2 tbsp. dijon style mustard
3 tbsp. parmesan cheese, grated
salt and pepper
parsley and lemon slices

1. In a small bowl mix the mayonnaise, mustard, cheese and salt and pepper to taste. Spread over the fillets.
2. Broil for 4-7 mins., depending on the thickness of the fish, or until the fish flakes with a fork. Do not overcook. Serve immediately. Garnish with parsley and lemon slices.

Crab Stuffed Red Snapper

Oven 400°F - 25 mins.
10 mins.

Serves 4

4 red snapper fillets
½ pound crabmeat
7 tbsp. butter
¼ cup onion, chopped
½ cup fresh mushrooms, chopped
½ cup saltine crackers, crushed
2 tbsp. fresh parsley, finely chopped
3 tbsp. flour
1½ cups milk
⅓ cup white wine
1 cup Swiss Gruyere cheese, grated
pinch of nutmeg
salt and pepper
paprika

1. Melt 4 tbsp. butter in a skillet. Add the onion and cook until soft. Remove from heat. Stir in the mushrooms, cracker crumbs, parsley, pepper and crabmeat. Spread this mixture over the fillets and roll up. Place seam side down in a buttered casserole dish.

cont'd...

2. Melt the remaining butter in the skillet. Add the flour, stirring and cooking for 2 mins. Slowly add the milk and wine, cooking and stirring until thickened. Season with nutmeg, salt and pepper to taste.

3. Pour the sauce over the rolled fillets and bake in 400° oven for 25 mins. Remove from oven and sprinkle with cheese and paprika. Return to oven and bake for 10 mins. or until the cheese is bubbly. Serve hot.

Cranberry Pottery

Red Snapper Creole

Oven 450°F – 10–15 mins.
Serves 6

This is a low-calorie delight.

2 pounds red snapper fillets
2 tbsp. butter
1 cup onion, thinly sliced
1 clove garlic, minced
1 cup green pepper, chopped
1 cup canned tomatoes, chopped
1/4 tsp. thyme
2 tbsp. fresh parsley, chopped
3 dashes tobasco sauce
salt and pepper

1. Melt 1 tbsp. butter in saucepan. Add the onion and cook until soft.
2. Add garlic, green pepper, tomatoes, thyme, parsley, tobasco and salt and pepper to taste.
3. Cover and simmer for 10 mins.
4. Butter the bottom of a casserole dish. Add the red snapper fillets in a single layer.
5. Pour the sauce over the fillets and bake uncovered in 450° oven for 10-15 mins.

Crispy Codfish

Serves 2

1 pound cod fillets, 1 inch by 2 inch cut pieces

Batter:

2/3 cup cornstarch
1/3 cup flour
1 tsp. vinegar
3/4 cup water
1 tbsp. baking powder

1. Mix cornstarch, flour, vinegar and water together. Add baking powder. Dip fish in batter and fry in hot oil at 375°F for 3-4 mins.

Maxine Nelson, Halfmoon Bay

Cod Baked in Sour Cream

Oven 400°F – 10-15 mins.
Serves 4 – 6

1 large onion, sliced
1 clove garlic, minced
6 large fresh mushrooms, sliced
2 pounds cod fillets
¼ cup parmesan cheese, grated
1 cup sour cream or yogurt
salt and pepper
paprika, parsley and lemon wedges

1. Butter baking dish. Arrange onions, garlic and mushrooms in dish.
2. Place cod fillets over the vegetables. Sprinkle with salt and pepper to taste.
3. Combine the cheese with sour cream. Pour over the fillets. Bake in 400° oven for 10-15 mins. until fish flakes.

Garnish with paprika, parsley and lemon wedges. Serve with baked potatoes.

Norwegian Poached Cod

Serves 4

2 pounds cod fillets
water to cover fish
1 medium onion, quartered
½ tbsp. whole peppercorns
salt to taste
butter, melted

1. Boil the water, onions and peppercorns until the onion is slightly soft.
2. Add the cod fillets and return the water to a boil. Immediately reduce the heat to simmer and cook for 5 mins. or until the cod flakes with a fork.
3. Remove the cod from the water. Serve with boiled potatoes and melted butter.

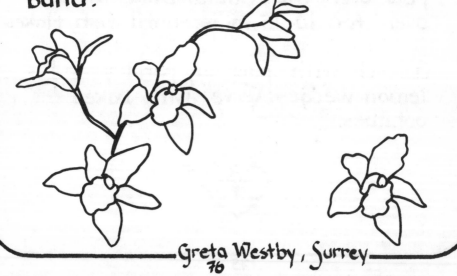

Pirate Rock Cod

Oven 450°F – 5-10 mins.
Serves 4

4 cod fillets
2 tbsp. butter
2 tbsp. lemon juice
½ tsp. thyme
salt and pepper
1 tsp. paprika
1 cup fine bread crumbs
6 tbsp. butter

1. Grease the bottom of a baking dish with 2 tbsp. butter.
2. Arrange fish in single layer and sprinkle with lemon juice, thyme, and salt and pepper to taste.
3. Mix the paprika with the bread crumbs and sprinkle over the fish.
4. Melt 6 tbsp. butter and dribble over the crumbs.
5. Broil about 6 inches from the heat until golden brown. Then bake in 450° oven for 5-10 mins.

Thormanby Baked Cod Fillets

Oven 425°F – 25 mins.
Serves 4

2 pounds cod fillets
4 tbsp. shallots, chopped
1 cup fresh mushrooms, chopped
juice of 1 lemon
2 tbsp. butter, melted
2/3 cup whipping cream
1 cup dry white wine
salt and pepper

1. Butter baking dish. Place the shallots and mushrooms in the dish. Place the fish on top.
2. Mix lemon juice, butter, cream, wine and salt and pepper to taste. Pour over the fish.
3. Bake in 425° oven for 25 mins., according to thickness of fish.

Clams Mussels Scallops

Clams

Mussels

Scallops

Clam Linguine

Serves 6

½ cup butter
3 cloves garlic, minced
¼ cup fresh parsley, chopped
½ tsp. basil
2 - 10 oz. cans baby clams
½ package linguine

1. Simmer butter, garlic and herbs for ½ hour.
2. Add clams and heat.
3. Cook linguine according to package directions.
4. Place drained linguine in bowl, cover with clam sauce.

Serve with crisp green salad.

Clam Pie

This dish is similar to chicken pie and makes an appealing addition to a buffet dinner.

pastry for topping
1 can (10 oz.) baby clams (including juice)
1 stalk celery, chopped
1 small carrot, chopped
½ cup onion, chopped
¼ cup butter
2 tbsp. flour
1 cup light cream or milk
1 large potato, cooked and cubed
salt and pepper
¼ tsp. thyme

1. Cook the celery, carrot and onion in butter until tender. Add the flour and stir, cooking for 1 min.
2. Gradually add the cream and clam juice, stirring constantly, cooking until thickened.

cont'd...

Add the clams and potatoes and remove from heat. Add salt and pepper to taste.

3. Pour clam mixture into baking dish. Roll out pastry and cover the pie. Brush the pastry with milk.

4. Bake in 450° oven for 10 mins. Reduce the heat to 375° and continue baking for 15 mins.

Creole Clam Sauce

(for linguine or fettuccine)
Serves 6

3 tbsp. butter
3 tbsp. olive oil
6 tbsp. flour
2 cups onions, chopped
1 cup green pepper, chopped
1 cup celery, chopped
5 cloves garlic, minced
1 can (6 oz.) tomato paste
2 cups beef stock
3 bay leaves
1/2 tsp. basil
1/2 tsp. thyme
1 tsp. chili powder
1/4 tsp. cayenne
1/4 tsp. black pepper
1 tsp. salt
2 - 10 oz. cans baby clams, (drained clam juice and water to make 2 cups)
1 cup green onion, chopped
2 tbsp. fresh parsley, finely chopped

1. In a large pot melt the butter and add olive oil. Add the flour and stir over low heat until light brown.

cont'd...

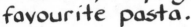

Add the 2 cups onion, green pepper, celery and garlic. Sauté until soft.

2. Add the tomato paste, beef stock, clam juice and seasonings and simmer for 45 mins.

3. Add the clams, green onions and parsley. Simmer for 20 mins. Remove from heat and let stand for 1 hour or more to let the seasonings blend.

4. Reheat gently. Serve over your favourite pasta.

Ellie's Boston Clam Chowder

Serves 4

This is a good recipe to make on a camping or boating trip.

8 slices bacon, chopped
5 medium raw potatoes, diced
¼ cup onion, chopped
1 cup water
1 tbsp. cornstarch
1 bay leaf
2 tsp. sweet basil
3 - 10 oz. cans baby clams and juice
¼ cup white wine
1 large can 2% milk

1. Fry bacon pieces until soft. Drain off the fat and discard.
2. Add the potatoes and the onions to the bacon. Cook for 2 mins.
3. Add the water, cornstarch, bay leaf and basil. Simmer for 10 mins.
4. Add the clams and juice, wine, 2% milk, salt and pepper. Bring to a simmer. Thicken with additional cornstarch if required. Serve with crackers or french bread.

Eleanor Lenz, Halfmoon Bay

Jeannie's Boston Clam Chowder

Serves 4

5 slices bacon, chopped
4 tbsp. onion, finely chopped
1 large raw potato, cubed
salt and white pepper
4 tbsp. butter
4 tbsp. flour
3-4 cups milk
1 can (10 oz.) baby clams, including
  juice

1. Cook bacon, onion and potatoes in frying pan until the bacon and onion are soft, but not browned. Add salt and pepper to taste. Set aside.
2. In a large pot melt the butter. Add the flour and stir and cook for 2 mins.
3. Gradually add the milk, cooking until desired thickness.
4. Add the bacon mixture along with the clams and juice. Simmer for about 15 mins until the potatoes are done.

—Jeannie Mercer, Buccaneer Marina

Lauren's Herbed Clams

Serves 4

2 cloves garlic, minced
3 tbsp. olive oil
2 tsp. sweet basil
1 tbsp. fresh parsley, chopped
1 tsp. oregano
1/4 tsp. cayenne (optional)
2 tbsp. black beans, rinsed and mashed (optional)
2 tbsp. dry white wine
4 dozen butter clams in shells, cleaned

1. Sauté the garlic in olive oil. Add the herbs and cook for 1 min.
2. Add the wine and clams. Cover the pot and bring to a boil. Cook until the shells are open, about 3-5 mins. Discard any unopened shells. Serve immediately with french bread.

Lauren Armstrong, Powell River

Marty Callaghan's Red Clam Chowder

Serves 8

Best served the next day.

6 slices bacon, chopped
3 small onions, chopped
3 tbsp. flour
1 can (10 oz.) baby clams
2 - 28 oz. cans stewed tomatoes
3 carrots, chopped
3 celery sticks, chopped
2-3 cups raw potatoes, chopped
¼ cup green pepper, chopped
½ bay leaf
¼ cup ketchup
3 tbsp. butter

1. Fry the bacon until cooked but not crisp. Remove from pan.
2. Add the onions to the bacon drippings and cook slowly for 5 mins.
3. Sprinkle the flour over the onions and blend.
4. Drain the clams and tomatoes and add water to make 4 cups of liquid.
5. Heat the liquid and onion mixture in a large pot.

cont'd...

6. Add the vegetables, bay leaf and ketchup. Cover the pot and simmer until the vegetables are cooked.
7. Add the clams, bacon and butter and simmer for ½ hour. Serve with french bread.

Madeira Park Mussels Mariniere

(mussels steamed in wine)
Serves 4-6

4 pounds fresh mussels
1 cup dry white wine
4 shallots, chopped (or green onions)
½ cup fresh parsley, chopped
2 cloves garlic, minced
2 tsp. lemon juice
1 bay leaf
1 tsp. thyme
½ tsp. salt
¼ tsp. pepper

1. Scrub mussels, using a stiff brush, under cold running water.
2. Place all the ingredients in a large pot. Cover and bring to a boil. Steam the mussels for 4-5 mins. over medium heat, shaking the pot a few times. Discard any mussels that remain closed.
3. Serve in large soup bowls with crisp french bread.

Eat the mussels from the shell.

Mussels Florentine

Serves 6

An exciting first course for a seafood dinner.

4 dozen mussels, scrubbed
8 cloves garlic, minced
10 ounces fresh spinach, cooked and
   drained
1 cup fresh basil, chopped
2 tbsp. lemon juice
½ tsp. dill
¼ cup fresh parsley, finely chopped
½ tsp. salt
3/4 – 1 cup mayonnaise

1. Place the mussels in a large pot
   with the garlic and 1 inch of water.
   Cover, bring to a boil and cook for
   2-5 mins. or until the mussels
   open. Remove the mussels with a
   slotted spoon and discard any that
   do not open. Remove the top shell
   from each mussel and discard. Strain
   the liquid and reserve the garlic.
2. Sprinkle the garlic over the mussels
   in the half shell. Place the mussels
   on a baking sheet and refrigerate.
cont'd...

3. In a food processor purée the spinach, basil, lemon juice, dill, parsley and salt. Add only enough mayonnaise to make a thick sauce.

4. At serving time, place a spoonful of sauce on each mussel. Serve.

Mussels Linguine

Serves 4

1 pound linguine, cooked to package
  directions and drained
1 cup dry white wine
3 dozen mussels, scrubbed
1/4 cup olive oil
6 cloves garlic, minced
1 tsp. basil
1 tsp. oregano
1/4 tsp. red pepper flakes
3 tbsp. fresh parsley, chopped
salt and pepper

1. Heat the wine in large pot to boil. Add the mussels, cover and cook for 3-5 mins. Discard any that do not open. Remove the mussels from the shells and set aside. Strain the cooking liquid and reserve.
2. Heat the oil in a pan. Add the garlic and sauté until golden. Add the spices and parsley. Add the reserved cooking liquid and bring to a boil, then simmer for 10 mins.
3. Stir in the mussels and salt and pepper to taste. Pour over the cooked pasta, mix and serve immediately.

Redrooffs Mussels

Serves 4

4 dozen mussels, scrubbed
3 cloves garlic, minced
3 tbsp. fresh parsley, finely chopped
3 green onions, chopped
6 peppercorns
1 cup dry white wine
1½ cups whipping cream
salt

1. In a large pot combine the mussels, garlic, parsley, onions, peppercorns and wine. Bring to a boil and cover, cooking for about 3 mins. until the mussels open. Remove the mussels with a slotted spoon, and set aside. Discard any that do not open.
2. To the liquid in the pot add the cream and salt to taste, and cook until thick. Be careful that the cream doesn't burn.
3. Place the mussels in large individual bowls and pour the sauce overall. Sprinkle with parsley.

Preheat the broiler
Serves 2

2 quarts mussels, soaked and scrubbed
2 tbsp. green onion, finely chopped
1 tbsp. fresh dill
2 tbsp. butter, melted
2 cups Gouda cheese, grated

1. Steam the mussels in boiling water until open, about 3 mins. Discard any that do not open. Break off and discard the top shells of the mussels. Arrange the mussels in the bottom shells in a shallow baking dish.
2. Mix the onion, dill and butter and spoon over the mussels.
3. Sprinkle the mussels with the cheese and broil 4-6 inches from the heat for 5 mins. or until the cheese is melted and golden.

Coquilles St. Jacque

Oven 400°F – 10 mins.
Serves 8

1 cup dry white wine
3 green onions, minced
1 pound scallops
½ pound fresh mushrooms, sliced
3 tbsp. butter
3 tbsp. flour
1 ½ cups light cream
salt to taste
1 tbsp. licorice liquor
2 tbsp. fresh parsley, chopped
parmesan cheese
mashed potatoes (optional)

1. Combine wine and onions and bring to a boil. Add scallops and mushrooms and cook for 1 min. Lift out scallops, mushrooms and onion and set aside. Boil liquid until reduced to ¼ cup.
2. Make sauce by melting the butter, add flour, cream and salt and cook until thick. Remove from heat and add the liquor.

cont'd ...

3. Add the reduced liquid, parsley and the scallop mixture. Blend well. Pour into scallop shells. Sprinkle with parmesan cheese. Pipe around edge with mashed potatoes.
4. Bake in 400° oven for 10 mins. or until bubbly.

Pacific Scallop Casserole

Oven 450°F – 20 mins.
Serves 4

1 pound scallops
2 tbsp. green onion, chopped
1 can (10 oz.) cream of mushroom soup
¼ cup dry white wine
¼ cup fine bread crumbs, buttered

1. Place scallops and onions in casserole.
2. Mix soup and wine and pour over scallops. Top with bread crumbs.
3. Bake in 450° oven for 20 mins. or until bubbly.

Scallops with Green Fettuccine

Serves 4

This is very quick and easy to prepare.

1½ pounds green fettuccine
2 tbsp. butter
1 cup fresh parsley, chopped
2 green onions, finely chopped
1 clove garlic, minced
½ cup dry white wine
1 pound scallops
1 cup milk
½ cup whipping cream
1 cup parmesan cheese, grated
pinch of nutmeg
salt and pepper

1. Melt 2 tbsp. butter in a saucepan. Add ¼ cup parsley, onion and garlic and cook for 2 mins. over medium heat.
2. Add the wine and cook until reduced to 6 tbsp. liquid.
3. Add the scallops and cook, stirring, for 1 min.

cont'd ...

4. Add the milk and cream and simmer for 2 mins.
5. Remove from the heat and add the parmesan cheese, 1/2 cup parsley, nutmeg and salt and pepper to taste. Keep warm.
6. Cook the fettuccine according to package directions. Drain and toss with 2 tbsp. butter. Place in dish Pour the scallop sauce over and toss lightly. Sprinkle with remaining parsley and parmesan cheese. Serve hot.

Stillwater Seviche

(marinated scallops)
Serves 8

2 pounds scallops
½ cup green or sweet red pepper, thinly sliced
½ cup purple onion, thinly sliced
2 tomatoes, chopped
4 tbsp. fresh parsley, chopped
2 cloves garlic, minced
2 tsp. brown sugar
½ tsp. tobasco sauce
salt and pepper to taste
2 cups fresh lime juice
½ cup lemon juice

1. Combine all the ingredients in a deep bowl. Cover and refrigerate for at least 5 hours. Stir occasionally.
2. Serve in individual bowls.

You may garnish with avacado slices and parsley.

Seafood Combinations

Seafood Combinations

Algerine Shrimp and Clam Sauce

(for linguine or fettuccini)
Serves 4

1 pound large shrimp, shells on
2 cups dry white wine
2 cans (10 oz.) clams, chopped, drained
  and juices reserved
½ cup additional clam juice
4 tbsp. butter
1 clove garlic, minced
4 tbsp. flour
6 ounces cream cheese, room
  temperature
salt and pepper
parmesan cheese
parsley

1. Bring the wine to a boil. Add the
   shrimp and cook until the shells are
   pink, about 3-4 mins. Remove the
   shrimp and shell, setting shrimp aside.
   Reserve the liquid.
2. Add the reserved clam juice plus
   the ½ cup additional clam juice to
   the wine. Boil for 5 mins. to reduce
   liquid by half. Set aside.

cont'd...

3. Melt the butter in a saucepan. Add the garlic and sauté for 1 minute. Add the flour and cook for 3 mins., stirring constantly.
4. Add the clam wine juice mixture and cook, stirring constantly, until thickened.
5. Whisk in the cheese until smooth. If the sauce is too thick add more clam juice.
6. Fold in the clams and shrimp and heat through. Add salt and pepper to taste.
7. Serve over cooked pasta of your choice. Sprinkle with parmesan cheese and parsley.

Bouillabaisse

Serves 8-10

Have guests join in the fun of making this casual dish. Use fingers to eat the shellfish and have large napkins available.

½ cup olive oil
1 cup leeks, coarsely chopped
1 cup onions, finely chopped
2 cups tomato sauce
3 cups tomatoes, chopped
1 tsp. thyme
½ cup fresh parsley, finely chopped
2 bay leaves
2 cups dry white wine
4 cups fish stock
salt and pepper
4 tbsp. butter
1 tbsp. flour
4 dozen clams, scrubbed
2 quarts mussels, scrubbed
1½ tsp. whole saffron
3 pounds fresh firm fish steaks (cod, snapper or salmon) cut into large chunks

cont'd...

3 dozen fresh prawns, shells on
10 crab legs, cracked

1. Heat the oil in a large pot. Add the leeks and onions and cook until soft.
2. Add the tomato sauce, tomatoes, thyme, parsley, bay leaves, wine, fish stock and salt and pepper to taste. Simmer for 20 mins. (You may prepare to this point and refrigerate until the next day. Return to simmer before proceeding.)
3. Blend softened butter and flour and blend into the tomato mixture.
4. Add the clams, mussels and saffron. Simmer for 5 mins.
5. Add the fish, prawns and crab and simmer another 5 mins. Do not overcook.
6. Serve in large bowls. Accompany with french bread and a dry red wine.

BC Canada

Serves 6

Be flexible when buying the seafood for this recipe – if one is not available buy another. The sauce may be made up to 2 days before serving. Reheat the sauce to boiling before adding the fish.

¼ cup olive oil
2 tbsp. butter
2 medium onions, chopped
4 cloves garlic, minced
½ pound fresh mushrooms, whole
1 can (28 oz.) Italian plum tomatoes
1 cup tomato sauce
1 green pepper, chopped
1 bay leaf
1 tsp. basil
¼ tsp. oregano
¼ tsp. thyme
½ cup lemon juice
2 cups dry red wine
2 pounds firm fleshed fish, halibut
    or red snapper, cut in chunks
½ pound scallops
2 dozen large prawns, shells on

cont'd...

1 Dungeness crab, cracked
1 dozen clams
1 dozen mussels, scrubbed
1 lemon, sliced

1. In a large pot heat the oil and butter. Add the onions and garlic and cook slowly for about 5 mins. Do not brown. Add the mushrooms and cook for 3 mins.
2. Add the tomatoes, tomato sauce, green pepper, bay leaf, basil, oregano, thyme, lemon juice and wine and stir. Bring to a boil, then reduce to a simmer for 1 hour. Taste and adjust the seasonings to your taste.
3. Twenty minutes before serving add the 2 pounds of fish. Simmer for 10 mins. Add the scallops, prawns, crab, clams and mussels and sliced lemon. Cover and simmer until the clams and mussels open, about 3-5 mins. Discard any clams and mussels that do not open.

Serve with plenty of sourdough bread and a dry red wine.

Crispy Batter

This recipe may be used when deep frying seafoods.

2/3 cup cornstarch
1/3 cup flour
1 tsp. vinegar
water
1 tbsp. baking powder

1. Combine the cornstarch, flour and vinegar. Add enough water to make a medium thick pancake batter.
2. Heat vegetable oil in deep fryer to 375°F.
3. Add the baking powder to the batter. Dip fish chunks in batter, fry for 3-4 mins. until golden brown. Drain on paper towels and serve warm.

— Myrtle Cunningham, Powell River

Deep Fried Squid

Good for a party snack.

2 pounds squid, cleaned
garlic salt
1 cup fine breadcrumbs
1 cup flour

1. Separate the squid head from the legs and body. Cut head crosswise in 1/4 inch rings. Drain all on paper towelling. Sprinkle with garlic salt.
2. Mix the breadcrumbs and flour together. Roll the squid in this mixture.
3. Heat vegetable oil in deep fryer to 375°F. Fry the squid for about 30 seconds. Remove from oil and drain on paper towels. Serve immediately.

Fresh Tuna with Tomato Sauce

Serves 6

Fresh or frozen tuna may be used in this recipe.

1 tbsp. butter
6 tomatoes, sliced
¼ cup onion, finely chopped
1 cup fresh mushrooms, sliced
½ cup white wine
½ cup chicken consommé
3 tbsp. butter
salt and pepper
2 pounds tuna, sliced 1 inch thick
½ cup fresh parsley, chopped

1. Melt 1 tbsp. butter in saucepan, add tomatoes, onion and mushrooms and sauté briefly.
2. Add the wine and consommé and simmer for 20 mins.
3. Meanwhile, brown the tuna in 3 tbsp. butter, using a large skillet.
4. Add the sauce to the fish, cover and simmer until the tuna flakes with a fork, about 15-20 mins. Add salt and pepper to taste.

cont'd...

Continued

5. Place tuna on a platter. Simmer sauce to desired thickness and pour over the tuna. Sprinkle with parsley and serve.

Howe Sound Fish Stock

Yields 3 quarts

This stock may be frozen in 1 cup portions for later use.

2 tbsp. butter
½ cup carrots, chopped
1 cup celery, chopped
2 cups onion, chopped
10 cups water
1 cup dry white wine
12 peppercorns
8 sprigs parsley
2 bay leaves
1 tsp. dried thyme
bones and heads (gills removed) of 6 to 8 non-oily fish such as sole or cod

1. Cook the vegetables in butter until tender.
2. Add all ingredients to stock pot and bring to a boil. Simmer for 35 to 45 mins.
3. Strain through cheese cloth and refrigerate or freeze.

Lord Jim's Paella

Oven 450°F
Serves 4

This is a very popular item on the menu at Lord Jim's Lodge. If there is no paella dish available, a large frying pan or wok may be used.

1 cup vegetable oil
1 small frying chicken, cut into small pieces
1 small onion, chopped
6 ounce garlic sausage, parboiled in water, skin removed then cut into chunks
3 cups Uncle Ben's rice
5 cups hot water
2 - 19 oz. cans Hunts Italian Sauce
1 tsp. garlic, chopped
1 tsp. saffron
1 cup frozen peas
salt and pepper
1/2 pound salmon, cut into 8 portions
15 mussels in shells, scrubbed
15 clams in shells, scrubbed

cont'd...

15 prawns, shelled and deveined
6 ounces baby shrimp, shelled

1. In a large paella pan, add oil and heat. Add the chicken and fry until brown. Add the onion, garlic sausage and cook briefly.
2. Remove the oil. Set aside the chicken and garlic sausage. Keep the onion in the pan and add rice, water, Italian sauce, garlic, saffron, peas and salt and pepper to taste. Mix well, cover and cook for 20-25 mins. over medium heat, stirring every 5 mins. Remove from heat and stir. Add salmon, chicken, mussels, clams, prawns, shrimp and garlic sausage. Arrange in dish, cover and bake in 450° oven until the rice is fully cooked.

Lord Jim's Lodge, Halfmoon Bay

Marinade for Barbequed Fish

Yields 2 cups

½ pound butter
2/3 cup beer, room temperature
6 tbsp. ketchup
6 tbsp. lemon juice
4 tbsp. Worcestershire sauce
grated zest of 1 lemon
½ tsp. ground black pepper

1. Melt the butter. Stir in the remaining ingredients. Cool to room temperature.
2. Marinate the fish for at least 1 hour before barbequing. Use the marinade for basting.

Scallops and Shrimp Au Gratin

Oven 375°F - 25-30 mins.
Serves 6

1 pound bay scallops
1 pound shrimp, shelled
5 tbsp. butter
3 green onions, finely chopped
1 clove garlic, minced
1 cup fresh mushrooms, sliced
1/4 cup flour
1 tbsp. fresh parsley, finely chopped
3/4 cup dry white wine
3/4 cup light cream
2 cups Monterey Jack cheese, grated
salt and pepper
1 can (8 oz.) artichokes, drained
1/4 cup fine bread crumbs

1. Cook the scallops in boiling water for 1 minute. Drain well.
2. Melt the butter in a large pan. Add the onion and garlic and sauté for 2-3 mins. over medium heat. Add the mushrooms and cook for 2 mins.
3. Add the flour and parsley and stir until well blended.

cont'd...

4. Add the wine and cream and cook and stir until thickened.
5. Add half the cheese and salt and pepper to taste. Stir until smooth.
6. Add the seafood and artichokes and mix.
7. Pour into buttered baking dish. Top with the remaining cheese and breadcrumbs. Bake in 315° oven for 25-30 mins. until bubbly and light brown.

Squid in Wine Sauce

½ cup olive oil
1 clove garlic, minced
½ cup green onions, chopped
½ cup fresh mushrooms, sliced
½ cup dry white wine
½ cup tomato sauce
salt and pepper
1 pound squid, cleaned and skinned
flour
vegetable oil for deep frying

1. Heat the oil in a saucepan. Add the garlic, onions and mushrooms and sauté lightly.
2. Add the wine, tomato sauce and salt and pepper to taste. Simmer for 30 mins.
3. Meanwhile, dip the squid in flour and shake off the excess. Deep fry squid in 375°F vegetable oil, until golden. Drain and add to the simmering sauce. Cook briefly to blend the flavours. (Long cooking will toughen the squid.) Serve immediately.

Sunset Coast Marine Seafood Lasagne

Oven 350°F - 45 mins.
Serves 6 - 8

12 lasagne noodles, cooked to package directions
2 tbsp. butter
1 cup onions, chopped
1 package cream cheese (8 oz.)
1½ cups creamed cottage cheese
2 eggs, beaten
2 tsp. basil
½ tsp. salt
⅛ tsp. pepper
2 - 10 oz. cans mushroom soup
⅓ cup milk
⅓ cup dry white wine or dry vermouth
1 can (5 oz.) crabmeat
1 pound shrimp, cooked
¼ cup parmesan cheese, grated
½ cup sharp cheddar cheese, grated

1. Melt the butter in a large pan. Add the onions and cook until tender.
2. Mix in all the other ingredients except the parmesan and cheddar cheese.

cont'd...

3. Layer the noodles, seafood mixture and cheese in a casserole dish. Repeat the layer.
4. Bake in 350° oven for 45 mins.

Sunshine Coast Seafood Casserole

¼ cup butter
1½ cups long grain rice
½ cup golden raisins
3 cups chicken stock
salt and pepper
4 tbsp. butter
1½ cups fresh mushrooms, sliced
1 tsp. curry powder
½ tsp. ginger
1 pound fresh crab
½ pound fresh shrimp, shelled
¼ cup dry white wine (or sherry)
6 tbsp. butter
¼ cup flour
1 tsp. dijon style mustard
3 cups light cream
1 cup Swiss Gruyère cheese, grated

1. Butter a large casserole baking dish - 13 x 9½ x 2.
2. Melt ¼ cup butter in large saucepan. Add rice and cook slowly, stirring until rice is golden.

cont'd...

3. Add raisins and chicken stock. Bring to boil, cover and simmer 20 mins. Add salt and pepper to taste, and spread mixture in bottom of casserole dish.

4. Melt 4 tbsp. butter in saucepan, add mushrooms, curry and ginger and cook 3 mins. Remove from heat, mix in crab and shrimp and wine. Spread over rice mixture.

5. Melt 6 tbsp. butter in saucepan. Sprinkle in flour, mustard, salt and pepper to taste, and bring to boil. Remove from heat and add cream all at once, stirring to blend. Return to moderate heat, and cook and stir until thickened and smooth.

6. Pour over seafood. Sprinkle with cheese.

7. Bake in 400° oven for 25 mins. or until very hot.

Metric Conversion Chart

Volume

1/4 tsp.	=	1 ml
1/2 tsp.	=	2 ml
1 tsp.	=	5 ml
1 tbsp.	=	15 ml
1/4 cup	=	50 ml
1/3 cup	=	75 ml
1/2 cup	=	125 ml
2/3 cup	=	150 ml
3/4 cup	=	175 ml
1 cup	=	250 ml

Weight

1 oz.	=	30 g
2 oz.	=	55 g
3 oz.	=	85 g
4 oz.	=	115 g
5 oz.	=	140 g
6 oz.	=	170 g
7 oz.	=	200 g
8 oz.	=	250 g
16 oz.	=	500 g
32 oz.	=	1000 g

Oven Temperatures

250 °F	=	120 °C
275 °F	=	140 °C
300 °F	=	150 °C
325 °F	=	160 °C
350 °F	=	180 °C
375 °F	=	190 °C
400 °F	=	200 °C
425 °F	=	220 °C
450 °F	=	230 °C
475 °F	=	240 °C
500 °F	=	260 °C

Order Forms

Please send me:

___ copies of Sunshine Coast Seafood at $12.95 a copy. Plus $1.50 a copy for mailing. Enclosed is $ ___ .

name _____

street _____

city _____ province _____ postal _____

Make cheque payable to: Arbutus Bay Publications, #12 (Jolly) Secret Cove, RR#1 Halfmoon Bay, B.C., Canada, VON1Y0

Please send me:

___ copies of Sunshine Coast Seafood at $12.95 a copy. Plus $1.50 a copy for mailing. Enclosed is $ ___ .

name _____

street _____

city _____ province _____ postal _____

Make cheque payable to: Arbutus Bay Publications, #12 (Jolly) Secret Cove, RR#1 Halfmoon Bay, B.C., Canada, VON1Y0

Please send me:

___ copies of Sunshine Coast Seafood at $12.95 a copy. Plus $1.50 a copy for mailing. Enclosed is $ ___ .

name _____

street _____

city _____ province _____ postal _____

Make cheque payable to: Arbutus Bay Publications, #12 (Jolly) Secret Cove, RR#1 Halfmoon Bay, B.C., Canada, VON1Y0